MANIFESTOS FOR THE 21ST CENTURY

SERIES EDITORS: URSULA OWEN AND JUDITH VIDAL-HALL

Free expression is as high on the agenda as it
has ever been, though not always for the
happiest of reasons. Here, four distinguished
writers address the issue of censorship in a
complex and fragile world where people with
widely different cultural habits and beliefs are
living in close proximity, where offence is easily
taken, and where words, images and behaviour
are coming under the closest scrutiny.
These books will surprise, clarify and provoke
in equal measure.

Index on Censorship is the only international
magazine promoting and protecting free
expression. A haven for the censored and
silenced, it has built an impressive track record
since it was founded 35 years ago, publishing
some of the finest writers, sharpest analysts and
foremost thinkers in the world. In this series
with Seagull Books, the focus will be on
questions of rights, liberties, tolerance,
silencing, censorship and dissent.

Without ████

████ding religious orthodoxies, it ceases to exist. La███

███n cannot be imprisoned, or art will die, and with it, a little of what me

s human. What is freedom of expression? Without the freedom to offend

███ases to exist. Without the freedom to challenge, even to satirise all ortho

s, including religious orthodoxies, it ceases to exist. Language

and the imagination cannot be imprison

or art will die, and with it, a little of

what makes us human. What is freedom of expression

Without the freedom to offend, it ceases to exist. Without the freedom to c

enge, even to satirise all orthodoxies, including religious orthodoxies, it

ases to exist. Language and the imagination cannot be imprisoned, or

█████████████████████████

ression? Without the freedom to offend, it ceases to exist.

ression? Without the freedom to offend, it ceases to exist. With

o challenge, even to satirise all orthodoxies, including religious orthod

t ceases to exist. Language and the imagination cannot be i

prisoned, or art will die, and with it, a little of what makes us

human. What is freedom of expres-

sion? Without the freedom to offend, it ceases to exist. Without t

dom to challenge, even to satirise all orthodoxies, including religious

orthodoxies, it ceases to e███

CENSORING

the moving image

PHILIP (F)RENCH

JULIAN PETLEY

Seagull
BOOKS

LONDON NEW YORK CALCUTTA

Seagull Books

Editorial offices:

1st Floor, Angel Court, 81 St Clements Street
Oxford OX4 1AW, UK

1 Washington Square Village, Apt 1U
New York, NY 10012, USA

26 Circus Avenue, Calcutta 700 017, India

© Philip French, Julian Petley 2007

ISBN-13   978 1 90542 255 5

British Library Cataloguing-in-Publication Data
A catalogue record for this book is available
from the British Library

Typeset and designed by Seagull Books, Calcutta, India
Printed and bound in the United Kingdom
by Biddles Ltd, King's Lynn

CONTENTS

CENSORING THE MOVING IMAGE

PHILIP FRENCH, JULIAN PETLEY

When the noted UK film critic and scourge
of the censors, Alexander Walker, heard
that James Ferman, director of the British
Board of Film Classification (as the British
Board of Film Censors was renamed in
1985; BBFC) was a member of the committee appointed to celebrate the centenary of
film in 1995, he wrote a letter of protest to
the committee's chairman. The reply he
received referred to Ferman's probity, his
devotion to the cinema and the obvious

discourtesy that would be involved in seeking his resignation. A more robust response would have been to say that since its earliest days the movie industry has been in an unholy—or, as the American Catholic Church's Legion of Decency would view it, holy—alliance with the censors: that censorship has shaped the course of movie history and played a part in determining the language of popular cinema. It would thus be as unrealistic and disingenuous to refuse the censor a seat at the centennial feast as it would once have been to deny the public hangman an invitation to a celebration of British penology.

Even before the first films were projected for a paying audience by the Lumière brothers in December 1895, the police had been intervening in Europe and North America to prevent peep-show machines from showing such innocently erotic items as *Dorolita's Passion Dance*, which was withdrawn in 1894 from the Kinetoscope

Arcade on Atlantic City's Boardwalk. Whether there really was a sequence of flicker-cards or a few dozen feet of film called *What the Butler Saw* is, we believe, uncertain. But the title has entered the language and for good reason. It suggests three things: voyeurism, class and dangerously illicit activities observed by and revealed to an outsider.

In 1896, one year after the Lumière show in Paris, 50 feet of film recording a gentle kiss between May Irwin and John C. Rice, both middle-aged, from the Broadway play *The Widow Jones*, had US papers calling for it to be banned. The following year, the moral opprobrium focused on screen violence as exemplified in a string of films bringing championship boxing matches to the general public. Terry Ramsaye, who lived through the period, wrote in the first comprehensive history of US cinema, *A Million and One Nights* (1926):

One marked effect of the Corbett-Fitzsimmons picture as the outstanding screen production of its day was to bring the odium of pugilism upon the screen all across Puritan America. Until that picture appeared the social status of the screen had been uncertain. It now became definitely lowbrow, an entertainment for the great unwashed commonality. This likewise made it a mark for uplifters, moralists, reformers and legislators in a degree which would never have obtained if the screen had by specialization reached higher social strata.

Shortly after the turn of the century, a Chicago judge claimed that cinema was among the chief influences—bad, of course—on the juvenile offenders who appeared before him. His sentiments were echoed over 90 years later when the English judge in the James Bulger murder trial suggested that the juvenile killers in Liverpool had been influenced by the US horror movie *Child's Play 3*, though the local police could find no evidence that the children had even seen it.

What was it that the benign US inventor, Thomas Edison, and his French friends, had unleashed upon the world, and that had so rapidly led to a demand for its control? The cinema developed during a period of unprecedented social change and, broadly speaking, there were seven aspects that made it seem a threatening phenomenon. Rebarbative language and disturbing sound were added to the list 30 years later.

First, there was the very size of the image and the immediacy, the intimacy of the experience. Second, film opened up life socially, geographically, in time and space, transporting audiences to places unknown, hitherto forbidden, invented. Third, the violence and eroticism were palpable, yet

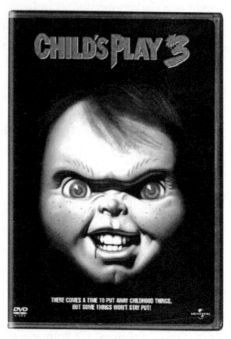

Child's Play 3 (1991 DVD case): British newspapers alleged, entirely without foundation, that this film had influenced the two boys who murdered James Bulger. The distributors immediately withdrew video copies of the entire series.

they left the audience unscathed. Fourth,
cinema offered an invitation to fantasize, to
dream, to revolt, and it is hardly surprising
that the Futurists and the Surrealists were
among the first to recognize its power. Fifth,
the movies rapidly became the most popular
leisure activity of the burgeoning urban
working classes, feared by the bourgeoisie as
a potential source of revolution and by inte-
llectual devotees of eugenics as a threat to
the future of western civilization. Sixth,
movie-going was a public activity that took
place in the dark, offering terrible tempta-
tions to innocent boys and girls. Seventh,
there were health and safety fears, some
real, some imaginary: fear of fire hazards
from unsafe buildings and highly inflam-
mable nitrate film; fear that the flickering
images might damage eyesight or induce
epilepsy; fear that these hot, fetid auditori-
ums could spread contagious diseases.

Some early opponents of cinema wanted to crush the new medium in the bud. In 1896, Herbert Stone, the eloquent editor of the Chicago literary magazine *The Chap Book*, wrote: 'I want to smash the Vitascope. The name of the thing is itself a horror. Its manifestations are worse.' Of the notorious Edison clip, universally known as *The Kiss*, Stone fumed:

> When only life size it was pronounced beastly. But that was nothing to the present sight. Magnified to Gargantuan proportions and repeated three times over it is absolutely disgusting. All delicacy or remnant of charm seems gone from Miss Irwin, and the performance comes near to being indecent in its emphasized vulgarity. Such things call for police interference.

Wherever films were made or shown, censorship boards sprang up. Around 1914, US producers united to oppose officially

constituted bodies, and the federal government refused to establish film censorship at
a national level, though this was precisely
what happened in virtually every other
country. But a major blow was administered
in a crucial judgement by the US Supreme
Court in 1915. Delivering the majority
opinion following an appeal by the Mutual
Film Corporation against censorship boards
in Missouri and Ohio, Justice McKenna
stated:

> It cannot be put out of view that the ex-
> hibition of moving pictures is a business
> pure and simple, originated and con-
> ducted for profit, like other spectacles,
> not to be regarded, not intended to be
> regarded by the Ohio constitution, we
> think, as part of the press of the coun-
> try or as organs of public opinion. They
> are mere representations of events, of
> ideas and sentiments published and
> known, vivid, useful and entertaining

no doubt, but as we have said, capable of evil, having power for it, the greater because of their attractiveness and manner of exhibition.

This decision, denying cinema the constitutional protection enjoyed by other media, was eventually reversed in 1952. But it set the tone for the way movies were to be perceived for decades, at least in the Anglo-Saxon world, and continues to do so into the twenty-first century.

Meanwhile, in the United Kingdom, censorship came in through the back door. The 1909 Cinematographic Act was introduced to license cinemas for safety purposes but was gradually extended by local councils and the courts to cover the movies shown in them. Extensive and frequently inconsistent film censorship by local authorities led to the creation in 1912 of the British Board of Film Censors; in effect, this was a joint initiative by the Home Office which viewed the still relatively new medium with suspicion, and the film industry itself, which was keen to appease local councils and thus to render their censorship activities redundant. In this it was largely successful.

Its second president, the ubiquitous T. P. O'Connor, Conservative MP, author and newspaper editor, served from 1916 until his death in 1929. During his reign, he made the film industry the acquiescent creature of the political establishment, a position from which it has yet to emerge.

Shortly after his appointment, O'Connor told a Cinema Committee of Inquiry that 'there are 43 rules and they cover pretty well all the grounds you can think of'. However, by 1931, T. P.'s rules, all of them prohibitions, had grown to over 90, many of which remained firmly in place until after World War II. These included: 'degrading exhibitions of animal passions', 'innuendoes with a direct indecent tendency', 'marital infidelity and collusive divorce', 'lampoons of the institution of monarchy', 'themes which are likely to wound the just susceptibilities of our allies', 'white men in a state of degradation amidst native surroundings', 'officers in British regiments shown in disgraceful light', 'horrors in warfare and realistic scenes of massacre', 'Bolshevist propaganda', 'incidents which reflect a mistaken conception of the Police Forces in this country in the administration of justice', and 'crime committed and condoned for an ostensibly good reason'.

As is clear from even this small selection, the prohibitions were concerned quite as much with politics as with sexual mores. Among the casualties were many of the great Soviet classics, as well as newsreels and feature films which attempted to draw attention to the horrors taking place in Nazi Germany. Indeed, such was the level

of suppression that, in 1937, the BBFC
president could announce to the Exhibitors'
Association: 'we may take pride in observ-
ing that there is not a single film showing in
London today which deals with any of the
burning questions of the day.' No wonder,
then, that Alfred Hitchcock had turned
away from political filmmaking for ever
when his plans to make a picture about the
1926 General Strike were rejected by the
BBFC.

It was some time before the US industry
produced anything as detailed as T. P.'s
rules. But when it came, the Production
Code was the most elaborate ever drawn
up, and sought to make US movies acceptable and inoffensive to juvenile audiences
at home and throughout the world. After
World War I, during which US cinema
began to establish the worldwide ascen-
dancy that today seems unassailable, Hollywood studios were coming under attack.

Their films and the behaviour of their stars were agents of a changing post-war morality that small-town America found threatening. Anti-semitism was part of this paranoia, directed towards a new industry largely created and owned by Jewish immigrants fleeing discrimination, hostility and pogroms in Europe. In 1920, newspapers across the country carried an item with a Washington DC dateline that began: 'The lobby of the International Reform Bureau, Dr Wilbur Crafts presiding, voted tonight to rescue the motion pictures from the hands of the Devil and 500 un-Christian Jews.'

The response of the Hollywood moguls was to invite Will H. Hays (1879–1954), a midwestern Presbyterian elder and postmaster-general in Republican President Warren Harding's Cabinet, to become president of the newly constituted Motion Picture Producers of America Inc. The year was 1921, his job was to put the industry in order and to preserve its leaders' fortunes.

He served them well for 43 years until his retirement in 1945 when he was succeeded by the diplomat and head of the US Chambers of Commerce, Eric Johnston (1896–1963), who changed the organization's name to the Motion Picture Association of America (MPAA). Johnston died in office and, after a hiatus, another recruit from Washington, President Lyndon Johnson's right-hand man, Jack Valenti (1921–2007), became MPAA president in 1966. Valenti retired in 2004 and was succeeded by a fourth Washington insider, Dan Glickman, a former Democratic Representative from Kansas, Secretary of Agriculture (1995–2001) and Dean of the Institute of Politics at Harvard.

Hays believed in the 'Ten Commandments, self discipline, faith in time of trouble, worship, the Bible and the Golden Rule', and declared at one of his first Hollywood press conferences:

Mae West (1933): sex icon and scourge of the
US Hays Office.

This industry must have towards that
sacred thing, the mind of a child, towards that clean, virgin thing, that un-
marked slate, the same responsibility,
the same care about the impressions
made upon it, that the best clergyman
or the most inspired teacher would
have.

He first introduced a system by which
the studios were to submit to the Hays Office the books, scripts and stories they were
considering for filming. Subsequently, he
sent out an informal list of what he called
'Don'ts and Be Carefuls'. The coming of
sound with its possibility for new verbal
offence, along with the influx of irreverent
new writers, many of them tough ex-jour-
nalists from big city newspapers, led to the
adoption in 1930 of a Production Code
drawn up by two midwestern Catholics, one
a Jesuit professor of drama, Daniel A. Lord
SJ, of St Louis, the other Martin Quigley, a

publisher of trade magazines whose empire
included the *Motion Picture Herald* and the
Motion Picture Daily. This Hays Office Code,
made mandatory in 1934, began with three
general principles: 'no picture shall be
produced that will lower moral standards';
'correct standards of life, subject only to the
requirements of drama and entertainment,
shall be present'; 'law, natural or human,
shall not be ridiculed, nor shall sympathy
be created for its violation'. This was
followed by eight double-column pages of
detailed applications, ranging from the
demand that 'no film may throw ridicule on
any religious faith' to various proscribed
words, including 'Fairy (in a vulgar sense)'.
The Code was designed to make every film
suitable for audiences of any age, and
remained in force until 1967 when the new
president of the MPAA, Jack Valenti,
replaced it by a system of certificated categories. This dramatic change was influ-

enced both by European systems of censorship and by European films which, with their greater freedom in the handling of sexual matters, were making serious inroads into the US market.

The Code helped change the language of Hollywood movies and cinema worldwide, as writers and directors argued and bargained with the Code's administrators, and invented stratagems to approach forbidden subjects and metaphors to express proscribed acts. Fireworks and crashing waves stood in for sex. Body language could suggest the taboo subject of homosexuality. A woman with shiny lipstick, or chewing gum, or smoking in the streets, or wearing plastic rainwear was identified as a prostitute. And the public came to take with a pinch of salt the come-uppance that the Code insisted be visited on glamorous villains. Yet there were whole areas of life that were ignored and distorted.

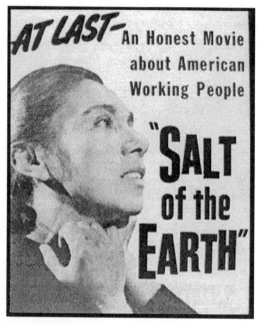

Poster advertising *Salt of The Earth* (1953): made by
filmmakers blacklisted during the McCarthy era and
long denied exhibition in the US.

The industry was opposed only to external censorship. It was the major studios themselves who, through their control of production, distribution and exhibition, decided who would make films and whose pictures would be distributed. When Hollywood bowed to the House Un-American Activities Committee (HUAC) and other McCarthyite witch-hunters in the post-World War II years, a group of blacklisted filmmakers produced *Salt of the Earth* (1953), an independent film about a miners' strike in New Mexico. They were harassed while on location by local and federal authorities, the leading actress was deported to her native Mexico and the completed film was denied exhibition in the US until the 1960s when it became a cult work among student radicals.

While this supposedly voluntary censorship was imposed in the US, movie-makers in the newly created Soviet Union were having their talents harnessed to the cause of ideology in a similar way. During the 1920s, artists were permitted considerable leeway to innovate; Vsevolod Pudovkin, Sergei Eisenstein and Dziga Vertov created a cinema that was revolutionary both politically and aesthetically. But with the coming of sound and the replacement of the enlightened Anatoly Lunacharsky by the philistine Stalinist cultural commissar, Andrei Zhdanov, Soviet cinema became rigidly controlled by bureaucrats and the doctrine of socialist realism was strenuously imposed on the nation's artists.

The European dictators of both Left and Right—Lenin and Stalin, Hitler and Mussolini—were fascinated by cinema and aware of its power. They therefore sought to exploit it in their own interests. In 1933, German cinema was taken over by the Nazis. Censorship of German-made films, however, was relatively rare, as it rapidly became quite impossible to make dissident

movies of any kind. One of the regime's
first acts was to establish the Reich Ministry
for Popular Enlightenment and Propaganda, with Goebbels at its head, charged
with 'the spiritual direction of the nation'.
This contained a Chamber of Culture,
whose task was 'furthering German culture
and regulating economic and social aspects
of cultural affairs'. This was further divided
into separate chambers, including a Chamber of Film, each of which was responsible
for one of the arts. One of the main func-
tions of these chambers, early in the
regime's history, was to facilitate the expul-
sion of Jews, Leftists and other *entartete
Kunstler* ('degenerate artists') from the cultural sphere, since only those who were
members of the appropriate chambers were
allowed to work in the arts at all. Trade
unions were, of course, banned. Addition-
ally, the 1934 *Lichtspielgesetz* (Cinema Law)
incorporated into the Film Department of

the Propaganda Ministry the *Filmprüfstelle* (Film Censorship Office), which had originally been established in 1920 and which, even in relatively liberal Weimar, gave legal protection to 'legitimate feeling for the fatherland' and discouraged the production of films which undermined 'Germany's reputation and standing'. More important, however, it established a new system of pre-production censorship, whereby all screenplays had to be submitted to the newly created *Reichsfilmdramaturg* (National Film Dramaturge). In such a thoroughly regimented and coordinated system, however, there was precious little to censor.

Sometimes, however, it is possible for artists working under oppressive regimes, such as French filmmakers during the Nazi Occupation and Eastern European cineastes of the post-World War II decades, to subvert censorship and censure by resorting to allegory, making movies with mythical subjects or putting them in historical settings. As in Hollywood in the 1950s, when the studios were reluctant to make political films or touch on matters of race, these issues were dealt with in the guise of westerns or science fiction.

As the first great mass medium, cinema provided the politicians and guardians of morality with the paradigm for censorship in the twentieth century. And, paradoxically in an era that has seen the democratic urge become central to social progress, there has grown up a culture of censorship, an expectation and acceptance of it. The least censorship—of films, as well as of the other arts and media—is usually found in confidently democratic countries that have recently experienced authoritarian regimes of the Left or the Right. In Greece and Spain, for instance, or Hungary and the Czech Republic, there is virtually no censorship of movies. But in countries that have not been exposed to such draconian treatment at the hands of the state, movies are subjected to pre-censorship that goes far beyond the methods of certification used to protect children.

In the UK, for instance, where the Lord Chamberlain's role in licensing plays was abolished in 1968 and prosecutions of literary works are largely a thing of the past, the BBFC has actually extended its influence, first into home video and then into DVD and digital games. It is true that the situation has become increasingly permissive (despite a lurching, three steps forward, two steps back method of advance). But the BBFC is still highly exercised about films that mingle representations of sex and violence, whether or not in an explicitly pornographic context, and the BBFC's statutory powers to license videos and DVDs for home use has led to films for domestic viewing being subjected to an elaborate set of rules based on prurient and class-based assumptions about the way people (and especially the proletariat) see and perceive films.

The simple fact is that at every societal level we have been inculcated with the idea that censorship is necessary—to preserve the social order, to protect 'us' from 'them' and to keep in check what the censorious regard as our baser instincts. Revolution, personal violence and sex forever lurk to disturb the status quo. And censorship is most evident in cinema because, unlike books, plays, exhibitions and TV and radio programmes, every film we see, every DVD we buy is prefaced on the screen or on the disc box by a certificate stating that the work has been examined and judged fit for us to see. This is a process in which the business side of the film industry—the major producers, distributors and exhibitors—is highly complicit. Directors, through influential sections of the industry. In particular, they were terrified—and not without reason—that what they regarded as over-liberal decisions by the BBFC would encourage local authorities once again to use their largely dormant powers to cut or ban films, powers which the industry had long thought the creation of the BBFC had rendered irrelevant. Thus, in a speech in March 1972, Kenneth Rive, then president of the Cinematograph Exhibitors' Association, an executive member of the British Film Producers' Association and a member of the Kinematograph Renters' Society called the then secretary of the Board, Stephen Murphy, 'the wrong man for the job', arguing that he was too liberal and too loath to cut. He added that as 'the film industry appoints the censor, so it is up to us to put our house in order by getting rid of him. He has got completely out of touch with public opinion.' Rive's speech was

A Clockwork Orange (Stanley Kubrick, 1971): after the film was accused (wrongly) by British newspapers of inciting copycat crimes, it was withdrawn from circulation in the UK by the director and re-released only after his death.

screenwriters and actors may indeed dislike
their work being bowdlerized, cut or even
banned, but what concerns the commercial
interests that govern the industry is, above
all, the maintenance and promotion of a
respectable image, one that is good for
business and that will not frighten off the
all-important (if much mythologized) 'family audience'. Thus, not only is it not in the
interest of the film companies to reveal
what the censor has excised for cinematic
exhibition or DVD release, it is not in their
interest to have their affairs looked after by
a censor considered too liberal by influential sections of opinion.

For example, in the early 1970s, the
BBFC passed in fairly rapid succession—
though not without a good deal of internal
dissent—a series of controversial titles such
as *The Devils*, *Straw Dogs* and *A Clockwork
Orange*. Although the first two were cut, the
films caused uproar among established
opinion, which in turn sent shivers of fear

prominently reported under the headline 'Murphy Must Go' by the trade paper *CinemaTV Today*, thus giving the Board's critics further ammunition in their campaign against it.

As the row threatened to spiral out of control, and to damage the industry as well as the BBFC, both sides declared a truce, but not before providing an unusually revealing glimpse into industry attitudes towards censorship. Significantly, Warners, who received the shock of their lives when Ken Russell first presented them with his masterpiece *The Devils*, and who self-censored it for a US release even more truncated than its UK one, have proved entirely unwilling to release theatrically or on DVD the uncensored 'director's cut' painstakingly assembled by film critic Mark Kermode and the film's original editor Mike Bradsell in consultation with Russell. Given the resurgence of Christian fundamentalism in the US and elsewhere, *The*

Devils, though a deeply religious work, is clearly thought by some to be even more controversial now than when it was first released.

One might suppose that there was enough official supervision. Sadly, the press, both popular and elite, tabloid and broadsheet, are among the first to demand tighter control of the movies, especially when it claims that the latest gruesome murder has been influenced by a recent film. It was claims such as this that led Stanley Kubrick eventually to withdraw *A Clockwork Orange* from circulation in the UK. This isn't confined to editorial writers and sensational columnists. All too often, movie critics demand that works that have offended be cut or banned. The late Dilys Powell, the liberal critic of the *Sunday Times* from 1939 to 1975, gave evidence for the defence when D. H. Lawrence's book *Lady Chatterley's Lover* was prosecuted for obscenity in 1960. Yet she claimed in 1948 that the innocuous gangster movie *No Orchids for Miss Blandish* should have been given 'a new certificate of D for Disgusting'. In 1954, she supported the BBFC's total ban on the Marlon Brando biker movie, *The Wild One*, stating, 'I am bound to say I think the Board was absolutely right.' In 1960, her opposite Sunday morning number on the *Observer*, C. A. [Caroline] Lejeune was so shocked by Michael Powell's *Peeping Tom* and Alfred Hitchcock's *Psycho* that she anathematized both and retired at the end of the year.

But perhaps most extraordinary of all was the letter to *The Times*, 17 December 1971, signed by 13 leading film critics, which complained about the banning of the Warhol/Morrissey film *Trash* but bizarrely coupled this with the suggestion that *Straw Dogs* should have met just such a fate. The critics in question were Fergus Cashin, John

Peeping Tom (Michael Powell, 1960): UK film critics' savaging of this film effectively ended Michael Powell's directorial career in his own country. It is now regarded by many, including Martin Scorsese, as a masterpiece.

Psycho (Alfred Hitchcock, 1960): unpopular with many critics both in the US and in the UK at the time of its release, this epoch-making film also caused intense debate in the MPAA and the BBFC. It was eventually passed with cuts.

Coleman, Nina Hibbin, Margaret Hinx-
man, Derek Malcolm, George Melly, Tony
Palmer, Molly Plowright, Dilys Powell,
David Robinson, John Russell Taylor,
Arthur Thirkell and Alexander Walker. The
letter is worth reproducing in full since it
provides such a revealing insight into UK
film critics' attitudes to censorship:

> Sir, A great deal of criticism, some of it
> well founded, some of it the product of
> prejudice and apprehension, is
> currently being directed at violence on
> the cinema screen, especially violence
> accompanied by extreme sexual agg-
> ressiveness. We acknowledge that it is
> probably not possible to establish a
> Quota System for either sex or vio-
> lence—or, indeed, desirable to do so,
> since in each case it is not the quantity,
> but the filmmaker's intention behind
> the display of these elements and the
> effects they have in the finished work

which ultimately provide the standard of judgement.

However, we wish to underline what many of us have already indicated and condemned in our separate reviews of the film *Straw Dogs*; that in our view the use to which this film employs its scenes of double rape and multiple killings by a variety of hideous methods is dubious in its intention, excessive in its effect and likely to contribute to the concern expressed from time to time by many critics over films which exploit the very violence they make a show of condemning.

Furthermore, we wish to draw attention to the now serious and growing inconsistencies of film censorship which passes for public exhibition such a violent film as *Straw Dogs*, yet so far has withheld any certificate at all from the film *Trash*. The film censor has been quoted as saying that it is his

Board's desire not to have drugs made
to seem a natural or acceptable part of
the contemporary scene which has
made it deny *Trash* a certificate.

We would welcome a statement
from the Secretary of the British Board
of Film Censors, or from his President,
Lord Harlech, who has so far remained
silent on the issue, even when the con-
tinued existence of his Board was being
called into question by several of the
signatories to this letter, as to how the
film censorship system can reconcile its
attitude to *Trash* with its attitude to
Straw Dogs. Is violence a more acceptable part of the scene, in the censor's
eyes, than drugs?

In 1996, a campaign against David
Cronenberg's film *Crash* began at the
Cannes Festival, where it was shown in com-
petition, and a demand for its banning in
the UK was made by Alexander Walker in
his report on the screening for the London

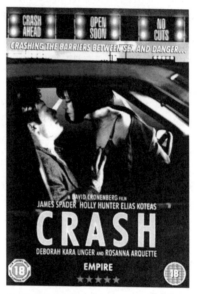

Crash (David Cronenberg, 1996): the object of a vicious smear campaign by Associated Newspapers in the UK, this film was passed uncut by the BBFC but banned by Westminster Council and certain other local authorities.

Evening Standard. He was subsequently supported by Christopher Tookey, film critic of the *Standard*'s sister paper the *Daily Mail*, and both papers attempted to pressurize the BBFC into banning the film. Not content with that, however, they also tried to force Columbia TriStar to withdraw it from distribution by urging their readers to boycott the products of its parent company, Sony. In spite of a highly personalized campaign against its staff, the BBFC passed the film uncut; meanwhile the boycott signally failed to materialize. However, the film was refused a certificate for public exhibition by Westminster Council in Central London. Elsewhere the BBFC's '18' certificate prevailed and it was possible to cross the line just north of Leicester Square and see *Crash* within the jurisdiction of Camden Council.

In the mid-1990s, a new form of censorship arose when several critics employed by British national daily newspapers called upon the minister for National Heritage to

investigate the financing from public funds
in Britain and Europe of movies of which
they disapproved, on either moral or aes-
thetic grounds—i.e. too sleazy or too arty.
Among the films so questioned were
Michael Winterbottom's harsh road movie,
Butterfly Kiss, and Dominique Deruddere's
Suite 16. For example, the *Sunday Express*
devoted a double-page spread to the latter,
entitled 'How Sleaze is Subsidised'. This
stated that '*Suite 16* was given a £500,000
(€735,700) subsidy from EU taxpayers. The
film cost £3 million (€4.3 million) and had
backing from The Netherlands, Belgium
and France, most of the money coming
from state bodies and lottery proceeds. But
the makers also picked up a handout from
Eurimages, the EU's fund for film production.' (In point of fact, Eurimages has nothing to do with the EU and is a scheme
funded by the Council of Europe.) Meanwhile, Alexander Walker noted in the *Stan-*

dard that 'the cash for this confused and squalid little item came from the taxpayers' own production company, the government-funded British Screen, and another public body, Merseyside Film Production Fund. In the sense that we all made it possible, we are all guilty.' Similarly, in the *Mail*, Christopher Tookey added that 'the distribution of this film is supported by the Media Programme of the European Community, so you may be doubly depressed to learn that you have put your hard-earned cash into it'.

Coincidentally or not, in November 1995, the UK government suddenly withdrew from Eurimages, arguing that the £5.5 million (€7.8 million) it had handed over to Strasbourg during the past three years as part of its membership of the scheme was an unnecessary drain on the Exchequer. However, since in the same period this had resulted in Eurimages investing some £12.5

Butterfly Kiss (Michael Winterbottom, 1995): this early work by one of Britain's most original contemporary directors was one of several films pilloried by critics from Associated Newspapers as examples of the profligacy of European film-funding schemes. Shortly afterwards, the UK government withdrew from Eurimages, the Council of Europe's film-funding scheme .

Suite 16 (Dominique Deruddere, 1994): dubbed a 'confused and squalid little item' by Alexander Walker in the *Evening Standard*, this film also featured in Associated Newspapers' censorious campaign against Britain's involvement in European film-funding schemes.

million (€17.8 million) in more than 60 films, thereby generating approximately £40 million (€57.2 million) in filmmaking activity, the purely economic argument for the withdrawal of its annual £2 million (€2.8 million) investment made little or no sense. In 1998, the newly elected Labour government announced that it intended to rejoin Eurimages 'when resources allow', but at the time of writing has still failed to do so, in spite of repeated lobbying by British filmmakers cut off from an important source of funding.

Subsidy schemes such as Eurimages, whether operating at a national or supranational level, are one of the very few means whereby the hegemony of Hollywood over much of the world can be at least partly offset and counterbalanced. Few today would argue for the imposition of quotas to stem the flow of Hollywood imports—indeed, these could be regarded as a form of economic censorship. However, the sheer extent of Hollywood's domination of the international film market—which in many countries, the UK most certainly included, has had the effect of significantly disadvantaging the production, distribution and exhibition of home-grown films—should also be recognized as a form of market censorship, and it is frankly both extraordinary and reprehensible that critics should be complicit in this process.

Looking back over a century of movie censorship, like Beaumarchais' Figaro, one laughs for fear that one might cry at the fatuity and foolishness of it all. For 100 years, audiences have been treated like untrustworthy children, artists as enemies of society. The BBFC refusing a certificate for over 30 years to Eisenstein's *Battleship Potemkin* in case it should foment mutiny in the Royal Navy. The same Board, at the height of World War II, holding up the

Battleship Potemkin (Sergei Eisenstein, 1925): poster by revolutionary artist and photographer Rodchenko advertising a masterpiece of revolutionary cinema banned from *public* exhibition (it could, in other words, be shown to only private groups and film societies) for 30 years in the UK.

distribution of *Western Approaches*, a documentary tribute to the Merchant Navy, because some torpedoed sailors in mid-Atlantic use the word 'bloody'. The French censors banning Stanley Kubrick's *Paths of Glory* in 1958 because it casts aspersions on the conduct of French officers in World War I, and Madame de Gaulle, 10 years later, attempting to have a film version of Diderot's *La Religieuse* banned because it presents the eighteenth-century Catholic Church in an unfavourable light. The Prince of Wales using his opening speech at the inauguration of the Museum of the Moving Image at the National Film Theatre not to celebrate the cinema but to call for the banning of horror films on cassette— the so-called 'video nasties'—to protect his vulnerable children, and getting applauded by the audience of newspapermen. The Soviet authorities, unable to make any sense of Andrei Tarkovsky's autobiographical film

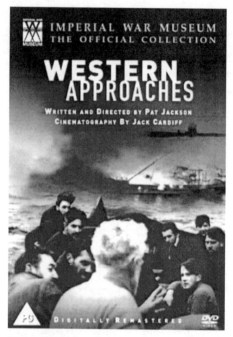

Western Approaches (Pat Jackson, 1944): a tribute
to the Merchant Navy held up by the BBFC for
strong language used in the heat of battle.

Paths Of Glory (Stanley Kubrick, 1958): banned by the French for its highly critical portrayal of French officers in World War I.

Mirror, banishing it to the cinema circuit
that served military bases. The New
Zealand censors approving the Joseph
Strick version of James Joyce's *Ulysses* only
for exhibition to single-sex audiences.

One could go on forever, as indeed film
censorship threatens to do. Fortunately,
there are also examples of filmmakers
running rings around the censors. In 1941,
in his directorial debut, John Huston got
'gunsel', a rare word (possibly of Yiddish
origin) for catamite used by Dashiell Ham-
mett in *The Maltese Falcon*, past the Hays
Office. The censors thought it underworld
slang for a gun-toting gangster rather than
a comment on the relationship between
Kasper Gutman and his homicidal assistant.
After the film was released, the censors'
misunderstanding of this obscure term led
to dictionaries giving its new primary meaning as 'a criminal carrying a gun'.

INTO THE TWENTY-FIRST CENTURY

As we advance into the new millennium, the
fear of the new and the challenging which
characterized the authorities' attitude to
cinema in the twentieth century still continues, on occasion, to exert a baleful influ-
ence. And just as in the twentieth century
television came to be viewed by the censorious in the same negative light as film, so in
the twenty-first the Internet and other new
forms of electronic image distribution have
been blamed for many of society's perceived ills. And while it is true, in general,
that the climate of the twenty-first century
in the west is more permissive than in the
past, and that classification now plays a
greater role than censorship in the activities
of bodies such as the MPAA and BBFC, the
limits of what is permissible continue to
preoccupy these bodies. In the UK, the
BBFC greatly extended its field of opera-
tions in the 1980s to cover video, and its
powers in the home-entertainment field

carried over seamlessly into the realm of
the DVD as soon as this new distribution
technology became commercially viable.
Today, however, the various technological
developments which usually go under the
name of 'convergence' have made it much
more difficult to monitor and control the
images which people watch in their homes
and offices, or indeed on their mobile
phones. In Britain, the government appears determined to make it illegal even to
possess certain kinds of pornography, in
whatever form; meanwhile the BBFC is
clearly concerned that the growth of film,
or of film-like content, on the Internet may,
simply by bypassing its classification system
altogether, put a question mark over its
continuing usefulness or even, indeed, its
existence. At the same time, however, as the
censors and classifiers undertake their activities in this much more complex world, they
may, paradoxically, find themselves acting

less as the guardians of public morality and more as the mediators of moral outrage generated by a public unfamiliar with the new technological developments and all too easily goaded into censorious reaction by a sensation-hungry, ill-informed and largely illiberal press.

So, is censorship of the moving image a threatened species as the century advances, or is it simply changing in nature?

IN CONVERSATION:

DAVID COOKE, DIRECTOR OF THE BBFC,

TALKS TO JULIAN PETLEY, 2 AUGUST 2007

JULIAN PETLEY. In recent years, the BBFC has become rather more liberal than it used to be and yet there haven't been any major press rows of the kind that used to plague James Ferman and his predecessor, Stephen Murphy. Why do you think that is?

DAVID COOKE. In my view, a lot of the explanation has to do with the decision to publish guidelines and to produce those on the basis of wide consultation with the public. Having admittedly come to this process fairly late and thus not being able to claim any credit for it, it seems to me that it was a very good idea that's had a whole load of quite profound and far-reaching consequences; in particular, it's enabled us to answer all kinds of fundamental questions, such as: is the BBFC there to lead public taste or opinion or is it there to reflect and be in line with it? We're now clear that it's the latter rather than the former because that's the whole basis on which the large-scale public consultation is done. It's enabled us to be a lot more predictable from the industry's point of view, because the people working in film and DVD distribution know exactly what our guidelines say. Many of them have become quite expert in the finer details of our individual cases and all our precedents, and so there are perhaps fewer surprises for them. That's probably true for the public as well, but one wouldn't necessarily expect the public to have, in all cases, as deep a knowledge of our practices as film distributors do. The big thing that's changed for the public, I think, is consumer advice or information provision and the fact that it's become much more widely available, under-stood and used—indeed, to the extent that some members of the public in some circum-stances may pay as much, or even more, at-tention to the consumer advice as they do to the rating. Our primary tools these days are the age rating and the consumer advice and not the cuts we make or don't make. Here, it's also important to note that we don't al-ways give the distributors the classification they want. I also believe that our recent an-nual reports are rather remarkable docu-ments in respect of their openness. It's quite something to have an official publication from an organization which, in effect, tries to give reasons for just about every controver-sial decision that the organization has taken during the year; this is quite a courageous thing to do and, in my view, really good in terms of making us accountable and open.

JP. Yes, if you compare your annual reports with the very thin and self-congratulatory documents produced by the Press Complaints Commission (admittedly rather a different kind of body), the difference between the two is extremely noticeable. Most sensible people would presumably agree that giving full consumer advice is a good idea, as is helping the people who submit films to you in whatever shape or form to keep within the laws of the land and thus avoid prosecution. However, some people still harbour a strong suspicion that the BBFC, over and above these objectives, is also overly concerned with wider matters of taste, decency and morality. Would you say that some of your decisions are sometimes influenced by non-legal factors?

DC. This is very difficult to answer because there are a lot of problematic concepts to get one's head around. The question of whether we're concerned with morality is a tricky one. There would be a possible argument that said we aren't and that what we are actually doing is operating a regulatory system where we are reading off decisions from the application of our guidelines, our policies and our precedents, and so morality doesn't actually enter into the process. And indeed it's true that, as far as adults are concerned, we do recognize very strongly the principle that provided they're operating within the law, provided questions of harm don't arise, they should be free to choose their own entertainment: we're not going to tell them which films are good or bad for them to see.

However, another way to look at it would be to say that we are inevitably working with values; that values and facts tend to get very much mixed up in some of the decisions we take; and that our whole approach is not a mechanistic box-ticking one but one which gives great weight to factors such as context, tone and so on.

JP. Let me try to make the question less abstract by taking one or two examples from

recent BBFC annual reports. In the case of
Paramedics, 'some of the more extreme and
detailed shots of gory and serious real injuries' were removed 'on a number of
grounds, including that exposure to these
kinds of images may encourage the devel-
opment of callous attitudes'. Turning to *Ter-
rorists, Killers and Other Wackos* and *Traces of
Death,* we find them described as 'a barrage
of sensationalist clips, the purpose of which
appeared to be prurient entertainment'.
The report adds that 'the works invited the
viewer to take sadistic pleasure in death, injury, mutilation and pain and encourage
callousness towards victims. In essence, they
had the effect of devaluing human life' and
reveals that 'cuts were considered, but the
essential difficulty of both works lay not so
much with any particular individual image
(most of which may have been acceptable in
a different, more serious context) but with
the manner in which the images were pre-

sented, and with the underlying, exploitative purpose of the works'.

Finally, in the case of the video game *Manhunt 2*, we read that it is 'distinguishable from recent high-end video games by its unremitting bleakness and callousness of tone in an overall game context which constantly encourages visceral killing with exceptionally little alleviation or distancing. There is sustained and cumulative casual sadism in the way in which these killings are committed, and encouraged, in the game. Although the difference should not be exaggerated, the fact of the game's unrelenting focus on stalking and brutal slaying and the sheer lack of alternative pleasures on offer to the games, together with the different overall narrative context, contribute towards differentiating this submission from the original *Manhunt* game.'

DC. All this does illustrate what I've said about the inevitability of facts and values being mixed up in our work, while at the same time we try not to lead public morals. There are really three main bases for our classification decisions. The first, which we've already mentioned, is legality, the second is harm, which we'll come on to, and the third is something that, at the moment in our guidelines, we call broadly based public acceptability. Some people would say that what you're really talking about here is offence, and we've asked ourselves in the past whether this third category, the slightly more taste-flavoured one, if you like, can be eliminated; we've reached the conclusion that it can't, really, because then we wouldn't capture the true, honest reasons for the things we do.

For instance, in the case of restricting the use of bad language at particular age ratings, you can't really have more than three or four 'fucks' at 12 and four 'cunts' at 15, and in the case of the latter they mustn't be aggressive either. My point is that you can't really in any clear way make or justify these decisions on harm grounds; you're doing it on some other grounds which have more to do with reflecting public wishes, sensibilities and so on. The other perception that we have is that quite often harm issues and more taste-based issues are very closely bound up with each other and they're quite difficult to disentangle. For example, concerning the issue of callousness in relation to these 'extreme reality' works that you mentioned, the thought is that there is a *risk* that these could be harmful in some sense. I don't necessarily mean harmful in the way that can be demonstrated through social science research, but also a sense that the public would think that we ought to be doing something about these works. The same sort of consideration applies to sexual violence. That's my way of trying to account for this kind of language.

JP. Clearly you take public attitudes and concerns very seriously. But do you take complaints a little less seriously if it's obvious that the complainant hasn't seen the film in question?

DC. We do take all complaints seriously in this organization and they tend to get much faster replies than they would from government departments or other regulatory bodies. They're quite careful replies too. But yes, of course, there's a difference between getting 50–100 letters or e-mails that have been generated by a template on a website and somebody reporting an experience which they themselves had when they went to the cinema. It doesn't mean that they don't both warrant a polite reply but maybe you might reply in a slightly different way.

JP. I would assume that most of the complaints you receive are from people who go to movies rated at below 18, and who then get rather more than they bargained for. Would this be correct?

DC. Broadly speaking, that's true, particularly in the case of blockbusters or near-blockbusters that are on the 12/15 border. Quite a few of these films do tend to come in around that borderline because the distributors are hoping for a 12A rather than a 15, because they want the bigger audience, but they're also hoping to have something that differentiates the work from a competitor. As a consequence, these are often quite difficult decisions over which we take a good deal of care. However, not surprisingly, there will be some people who'll think we've got it wrong and I guess the most famous recent case was with *Casino Royale*, which was definitely at the border between 12A and 15. We required some reduction to the torture scene to get it into 12A. It had express consumer advice referring to the fact that it contained a torture scene but we got around 100 complaints, although maybe 10 million people would have seen it while it was in the cinema.

JP. Now that the press is making less fuss about movies, and you haven't had a *Crash* on your hands, would I be right to assume you don't get so many complaints from people who haven't seen the film in question?

DC. It can still happen. My first big decision, almost three years ago, was Michael Winterbottom's *Nine Songs* and I got quite a lot of e-mails and letters from people who hadn't seen it.

JP. I'm surprised there wasn't more of a hoo-hah about that. Perhaps there would have been if the film had actually been enjoyable and erotic!

DC. Coming to it as a complete newcomer I thought it was a difficult decision, although it wasn't my decision alone and it was reached only after a good deal of analysis within the organization; as with all the most difficult cases, the BBFC presidents were involved as well. One of the reasons it was eye-catching was that it contained real sex and a lot of people assumed that there had been no real sex in a non-porn film before. However, as we pointed out in our press release, there *had* been examples going back to *Ai No Corrida* in 1990. It was a difficult decision because there were several issues, one of them being: what exactly were we dealing with here? This was a film by quite a famous director, something that wasn't going to be confined purely to the art-house circuit, and something that did raise quite challenging issues about what you were watching. Our argument was that: yes, you were watching some explicit images of real sex (although not quite as many as people thought they were seeing) despite which it wasn't pornography. Most people were probably convinced by that argument, although not everybody and, for them, ours would have been a contentious decision. Our argument was that pornography looks completely different—the whole thing is staged, framed and shot in a different way, there is a clear underlying rationale of producing sexual arousal, not just in little bits of it but throughout the work taken as a whole—and that what we had here was a very different beast.

JP. Let's come on to the question of harm. The Video Recordings Act [see Appendix 2] requires you to take into account when classifying a DVD any 'harm' this might do to a potential viewer, and any 'harm' that might be done to society as a result of people watching that DVD. How do you understand this notion of harm? I can understand, for instance, that if you showed a close-up of someone picking a lock or hot-wiring a car, then that could be seen as harmful. It's showing someone techniques that are criminal and anti-social, and in that sense it's harmful; but once we get beyond imitable techniques, I find the notion of harm, in this context, a difficult one.

DC. You can't possibly get far into this argument without looking at the state of the research and, as you and Martin Barker have pointed out [in *Ill Effects*], even the very concepts involved in the research are problematic. So it is a very contested area and from a regulator's point of view it's difficult to draw out of it very clear-cut policy prescriptions in specific areas. Some people say that there are no 'media effects' and that we should just forget about this way of thinking. Other people tend to put it differently and say that every time somebody thinks they've demonstrated an 'effect', somebody else comes along and raises questions about whether they *have* actually demonstrated it, and so argues that the jury is still out on harm and 'effects'. But we would want to say that you need a bigger world of possible harm concepts than simply the kind of things you can try to demonstrate through social science research. There are some kind of possible harm effects that you might conceive of which you could hardly even hope to get at through such re-search—long-term corrosive effects.

JP. For me it's the long-term that's most in-teresting, but I think this takes us into the area of media influence as opposed to 'effects'. I do believe that the media influ-ence people, but over a long period of time, in complex ways and in concert with, or in opposition to, all sorts of other influ-ences. It's not so much that these processes aren't amenable to social science research but that the research is costly and doesn't result in quick, eye-catching conclusions with obvious legislative pay-offs. However, work-ing with focus groups can be very rewarding in this area, and I know that the BBFC does make use of these.

DC. I agree with all of that, and so the con-clusion I would draw is that there may be other types of possible harm concerns that we might look at. We're also interested in what the public thinks we ought to look out for as being potentially harmful. That doesn't necessarily mean that we will derive very restrictive rules based on that, but there's this whole family of different things including, but by no means confined to, social science research. This results in our trying to derive pragmatic rules of thumb for dealing with possible harm risks, possibly in some circumstances conscious that we're taking a precautionary approach, although not being precautionary more often than we have to.

JP. Again, perhaps it might be helpful if we discuss a couple of specific examples, this time from the R18 category of DVDs, which may be sold only in licensed sex shops. As you know, 24 per cent of DVDs were cut at R18 in 2006 and two were banned outright in the last couple of years, *Severe Punishment* and *Struggle in Bondage*. Is the Board trying simply to keep within the law, or are other kinds of judgements operating here as well?

For instance, you say in the 2005 *Annual Report* that the Board has 'strict policies on material which combines sexual detail with activity which is illegal, harmful, abusive, or involves a lack of consent or the infliction of pain or injury'. Isn't this going to cut out a great deal of sado-masochistic (S&M) pornography, for example, which often depends on the *illusion* of lack of consent but is in fact perfectly consensual? Or, indeed, consensual sex, which is nonetheless pretty rough? Isn't this reminiscent of what the censor in Paul Hoffman's recent novel *The Golden Age of Censorship* wanted, namely 'an ideal censorial state in which nobility of purpose, morally good manners and rationality could be brought to bear on material blatantly ignoble, immoral, ill-mannered and atavistic'? Or of your predecessor James Ferman, who seemed to think that happy, jolly eroticism was OK but that anything stronger was problematic?

The Evil Dead (Sam Raimi, 1981): a cause célèbre of the 'video nasties' era, denied a certificate in uncut form and dragged before the courts on numerous occasions.

DC. Well, we wouldn't regard what we were doing as being in pursuit of the noble and avoidance of the ignoble! With R18s, two different but sometimes interrelated things are involved. One is that we are trying to stop them from breaking the law, which we are actually required to do by the terms of our designation. I think, to an extent, that distributors can be grateful, although they're not always. You do get some very tricky examples. One is urolagnia ['golden showers': sexual arousal that involves urine].

JP. Apparently juries are quite exercised by this, although personally I just can't understand why some people get so worked up about it.

DC. Quite a lot of people here who work on this type of film themselves question whether this is really a necessary intervention. But our concern here is not harm-based; it derives entirely from our understanding of the way in which the courts interpret obscenity. If they interpreted obscenity in a different way, then we would operate our practice differently. But when it comes to non-consensual or abusive stuff, that's different because that isn't necessarily going to fall foul of criminal law; there, the harm risk features more strongly in the rationale.

JP. OK, few would defend representations of genuinely abusive sex, but there's a big difference between these and representations of *apparently* non-consensual sex. Isn't it the case that in a great deal of S&M activity and imagery, a significant part of the thrill is precisely the convincing illusion of a lack of consent?

DC. We think that, although it's not always easy, we can distinguish a role-play from something which is genuinely abusive. The only thing we can go on is the on-screen evidence. We do indeed examine a certain number of S&M works, and we've talked to S&M experts and members of the S&M community, who have told us about good and bad set-ups, and some of the hard cases that we argue about in our examiners' meetings will be on this very issue: is there a real lack of consent, is it clearly a lack of consent? There have certainly been cases where a recommendation has come to me for intervention and I've said, sorry, I just don't believe this is a case of real lack of consent, this is role-play, and so we haven't intervened.

JP. Surely nothing less than the wisdom of Solomon is required here?

DC. I don't pretend these are easy judgements for an examiner patrolling the boundaries between R18 and breach of law. These can be incredibly fiddly and minute matters, but you have to try to base them on a rational set of principles. Anyway, a lot of the images which give us problems at R18 are not really from S&M works, and I wonder what you'd think if you'd been dealing with this kind of material for a month or so. There is a whole load of stuff, a certain amount of which I see, that is really nasty and in some cases it looks as though no human intelligence has been applied by whoever is distributing the work. For example, we're talking about gagging during deep-throat fellatio, with the woman being held in such a way that she can't possibly pull away, and so on. Some of this stuff really is quite unpleasant.

JP. This brings us on to the whole question of sexual violence, something about which the Board has always been concerned. For example, the 2005 *Annual Report* states that 'scenes or narratives that offer sexual violence as a pornographic pleasure, or which suggest that the subjects enjoy or deserve sexual assault, is of particular concern, even at "18" '. Media research in this area has tended to identify three possible harmful effects, especially when the victim is shown 'enjoying' the sexual violence: the stimulation of aggressive thoughts and fantasies; the cultivation of anti-female attitudes; and more aggressive subsequent 'behaviour'. My argument is with the research. Can one legitimately generalize from one person's particular responses to a particular film at a particular moment, which is what certain sorts of psychologists tend to do, to people's attitudes and behaviour towards real women in the real world? Some men do indeed have negative attitudes towards women, but it seems to me legitimate to regard certain kinds of pornography as symptoms, rather than causes, of those attitudes.

DC. It's clear that this is one of those areas in which the public still expects us to be particularly vigilant, but it's also clear that the research findings here are a bit more equivocal than they are in some of the other areas. I know these are contested and not clear-cut but there are still, as I understand it, some warning question marks hanging in the air. What we've ended up doing is deriving a policy on sexual violence which takes account of public concern and which, at its base, is concerned with whether watching certain kinds of images might or might not encourage sexual assault. Of course, we interpret that risk in different ways, and these may change over time; there have been one or two celebrated things that were cut on these grounds 10 years or so ago that we might now view in a slightly different way. Russ Meyer, for instance, comes to mind, and one of the questions there would be: how credible are such images in such a context? Is Russ Meyer really going to encourage people to commit rape? No, it doesn't seem very plausible.

An interesting thing about this policy is that it can have some counter-intuitive outcomes. I think if you asked people what we should do when faced with a rape scene, then, unless they'd reflected quite hard, they might well say that we should cut really shocking rape scenes. However, really shocking rape scenes can be highly aversive, so we tend not to intervene in those cases, as in the famous scene in *Irreversible* which the Board examined just before I arrived. What it can mean is that the material which we still cut may, in some senses, come across as being less strong than some of the material which we don't. There's a very, very shocking rape scene at the end of *The Great Ecstasy of Robert Carmichael* which we didn't cut because we thought it was aversive. Whereas we do still cut, for instance, the famous multi-tentacular rapes which you get in certain *animés*, rapes which you could say have much less impact because they're presented in a very cartoonish way but which, on the other hand, may set up collusive fantasies. The girls, incidentally, appear to change their ages quite alarmingly depending on what part of the work they're in. Quite often they seem to be enjoying it, and so there is a sense that we still ought to be cautious about what kind of impact that might have on people and that it's not giving a signal that rape is OK after all.

JP. Clearly you're worried that people might read off attitudes from films and take them into their own lives. But it does interest me that, on the one hand, the usual litany of names comes out in your *Annual Reviews*—Donnerstein, Linz, Malamuth, Check, Zillman, Bryan, Berkowitz and so on—but then, on the other, you commission research reviews from people such as Guy Cumberbatch, who regularly dismisses this stuff, and you also work with people such as David Buckingham and Martin Barker, who come with very different points of view. I wonder why you continue to appear to have such faith in Donnerstein and Co.!

DC. I wouldn't like to say I have faith in them any more than I'd want to say I have faith in Craig Anderson in the games area. I'm open to this material but also very conscious of the critiques of people like Guy Cumberbatch, and David Buckingham sits on our Council. We're lucky with the people we can go to for advice. It's rare for us to derive highly specific policy interventions from research because it's very difficult to do that. Maybe you're right, maybe the nearest we come to that is still in the sexual violence area, but in my view that's reinforced by knowing that the public wants us to be vigilant there. If we had better tools, we'd grab them. If the kind of research that you would like to see done actually existed then we would certainly want to have the results of that too.

JP. The trouble is that that kind of long-term research is pretty labour-intensive and thus quite expensive. It costs a couple of thousand pounds, for instance, just to put together a proper focus group. It's much cheaper to sit someone down in the lab with electrodes attached to them. And this also delivers the kind of results that the powers-that-be seem to want to hear.

Let's come to video games. What ingredients require a video game to be submitted to the BBFC?

DC. There are two broad factors. Most video games are exempt from our classification and so they are classified by the voluntary Pan-European Game Information (PEGI) system. We classify what we tend to think of as the top end, where the main distinguishing criteria are gross violence and the depiction of human sex organs. But there's also a very complicated legal artefact which has to do with the way the legislation is drafted. Again, even if on the face of it it's a 15 or a 12 or an even lower-category game, if it contains a lot of film-like footage then that can also cause it to lose its exemption. We have had a big hike in the number of games coming to us in the last year or so [298 were submitted in 2006], and for some the temptation is to say that's because there's more gross violence, but that may not actually be the case.

JP. When I read the BBFC's very interesting memorandum to the Department of Culture, Media and Sport Select Committee

hearing on New Media and the Creative Industries, I thought I detected a rather de-
fensive tone in some of the passages about
Ofcom [the Office of Communications, created in 2003]. In this age of media convergence, are you worried about Ofcom
encroaching on your territory?

DC. No, we didn't intend to sound that note.
We have a pretty good relationship with
Ofcom and meet each other on many different levels. If there was any element of
anxiety coming through, I think it's the
notion that we have a well-founded, open
system for classifying films and DVDs, but
only in the area our legislation covers. But
when you come to direct download distribution, most lawyers think, although this hasn't
yet been tested by the courts, that our legislation doesn't extend to that. Distribution
by download is happening at the moment,
although not on a very big scale, but you
can imagine possible scenarios where a
good deal of what we do simply migrates to

an area outside our statutory reach. That's where the anxiety comes in, and there are broadly two possible responses to this scenario. One of them is to say to the industry, look, you don't have to come to us in this area but you might still like to do so anyway, given the high profile of our brand and the degree of confidence in our detailed consumer advice. The other route is much more problematic, and everybody knows that. It's not to say, right, we want to regulate the Internet. But it is to ask if it's possible to define very tightly some limited area of DVD-like distribution that will actually occur through download and bring that within the statutory regulations. I don't know whether that will happen but we're exploring both routes at the moment.

JP. I can certainly see the attractiveness of the BBFC brand name and kite marks to certain multimedia distributors. But at the same time, I can't see that you can do much more than offer your services to such distributors, who aren't obliged to accept them. So the question then arises of whether you think there should be some pressure or even coercion from the government for them to do so.

DC. There are forms of co-regulation that might be interesting. Part of the difficulty in answering this kind of question is that it's such a vast universe that we're discussing. There are some people who might well come together and form a sort of voluntary club, but then there might be other people who they might not want to have in their club, or who might not want to join the club and who have absolutely no incentive to self-regulate responsibly at all. I don't know any country in the world that thinks it's cracked this issue and, in my view, the only overall conclusion you can draw at the moment is that maybe there has to be more than one answer and that there's no single way of dealing with it.

JP. The reason why I asked whether you
think it would be desirable for the government to be involved here is simply because
the BBFC memorandum to the Department of Culture, Media and Sport Select
Committee states that 'what is required is a
coordinated and systematic approach in
which the major new industry players and
the regulators come together to devise a co-
herent set of solutions. Such an approach is
unlikely to develop unless it is driven by the
government, the only authority that has an
overview across all aspects of new media,
technology and the public policy concerns
that underlie all types of media regulation.'
It also says that 'no one agency can provide
a single, readymade solution, and the diver-
gence of interests both among industry
players and between the industry and the
public make it unlikely that a satisfactory
regulatory framework will emerge without
the coordinating hand of the Government'.
This immediately made me recall the

rather unhappy circumstances surrounding the founding of the Internet Watch Foundation, when reluctant Internet service providers (ISPs) such as Demon were essentially coerced into joining a self-censorship regime by the police, no doubt with the backing of the Home Office, threatening to prosecute ISPs who had material on their servers which the authorities deemed illegal.

DC. Things have moved on a bit since we wrote that and there is now a forum that involves us, government departments, Ofcom and members of the industry. It's very complicated and this is all a developing area. Matters have also been confused by the changes to the European Union's Television Without Frontiers Directive [which has been revised to take account of new forms of media and has, in the process, become the Audio Visual Media Services Directive].

JP. Quite. You say in the memorandum that you'd like to see a 'systematic and coordinated approach' from the government in the new media area, but on the one hand the government has made it abundantly clear that it wants to criminalize people who download what it calls 'extreme pornographic images', and then, when our European partners do indeed try to introduce a degree of regulation of Internet content, it joins forces with the telecommunications companies in strenuously lobbying against such regulation, succeeding eventually in turning it completely on its head. So much for joined-up government! This kind of thing can't make your life exactly easy.

DC. We were basically just observers of that process so I couldn't really give you a take on all the twists and turns: I simply didn't follow all of them. As for the pornography legislation, we could see from our own experience why the government was concerned about this area. We knew there were some very nasty individual cases which they were concerned about so we had some sympathy for what they wanted to do. At the same time, we were extremely worried about some of the unintended consequences that might follow from legislation in this area. We did actually tell them that if they really wanted to tackle these kind of questions, maybe they should look at the whole question of the state of obscenity law and see whether they ought to start from scratch. But for reasons which I perfectly understand, they didn't fancy that very much! We're very pleased that they have included in the relevant clauses of the Criminal Justice Bill a provision which means that films with a BBFC certificate are taken out of the legal danger zone. Beyond that we'll follow its parliamentary progress very closely, and there are some points of detail on which we are in discussion currently with the government where we think they haven't got it quite right. I can't really go any further than that at present.

JP. Let's follow J. S. Mill and talk about the balance of harms. Isn't there a very real danger that in trying to regulate what I think is largely unregulatable, namely the Internet, in order to prevent what are, in my view, some rather vague and ill-defined harms to children, the vulnerable and so on, very real harms are done to people's civil liberties and human rights?

DC. We're always exercising ourselves about balancing acts of one kind or another. We often say that it's really important to understand that our decisions are not 'phone a friend' or 'ask the audience' decisions and are based on a whole complex of legal and other considerations. We do, as an organization, perhaps slightly paradoxically, want to give as much way as we can to freedom of expression because we think there are all sorts of goods that come from that; and the principles on which our guidelines are based reflect that because they are about trying to enable films to reach the widest audience that they can safely do. In the specific terms of the European Convention on Human Rights, do I think that freedom of expression goods are always going to outweigh the goods of protecting public morals and public safety? It varies from case to case, depending on what you're trying to do. We do care about film here and we do care about freedom of expression, so we don't want to interfere unless we feel we have to.

JP. You've talked a good deal lot about public expectation and public opinion. I don't want to sound elitist or snobbish about this, but in my view there's informed public opinion, the kind of public opinion which arises, for example, from the citizens juries which the BBFC has organized, and then there's uninformed public opinion which is usually, in my view, parroted straight from nonsense in newspapers.

DC. I know exactly what you're getting at but there may be a non-elitist way of formulating it. In my view, the fairly recent research that Sue Clarke [BBFC chief press officer] commissioned on our consumer advice presents quite an interesting case. It ended up giving us a good deal of useful practical information about how to do it and what traps to avoid; it also marked the death knell of the much-mocked 'mild peril' warning. This research told us quite strongly that we were being self-indulgent by using terms like that. One of the things that was very striking about this research was that the groups were made to write their own consumer advice, and when they tried to do this they found it bloody difficult. That's what I think you're getting at, the notion of being forced to think something through and actually produce a reasoned position rather than just a knee-jerk one.

JP. Yes, it is, but I was also suggesting that it's one thing to react to genuine public concerns about something and quite another to react to what are basically myths made up and peddled by newspapers and echoed by populist politicians. I know that the Board is composed of sane and rational individuals who are extremely well informed about film, but you know better than most that when MPs' postbags start filling up with letters complaining about this or that film, that must put you in a very difficult position. After all, the BBFC is designated as the body responsible for the statutory classification of films viewed in the home, and you could be de-designated if the government perceived you to be overly liberal.

DC. You're right, we can be de-designated and ultimately the government could legislate us out of existence. That said, as a regulatory body we are more independent and more distant from the government than most quangos or regulatory bodies, and noticeably more so than many of our colleagues in other parts of the world. The key test, in my opinion, is that no government funding goes into the organization, so there's no question of the government putting budgetary pressure on us, and the government plays no role in appointments either.

JP. What about Jack Straw not allowing Lord Birkett to be elevated from vice-president to president because he felt that the Board needed a less liberal head?

DC. I don't know about that, which was before my time. But what I can say is that since I've been here, and I would be surprised if my predecessor Robin Duval couldn't say the same thing, nobody in government, neither a minister nor an official, has ever said to me, privately or in public, that it would be jolly good if you could actually ban *Manhunt* or whatever. There really isn't interference of the kind that you might get in an executive agency or a body like that.

JP. No, I'm sure it doesn't work like that, any more than Rupert Murdoch tells Robert Thompson what to put into *The Times* every day. But if you look at the backgrounds of the top brass of the BBFC in its early days, you see that before these people came to the Board they were absolutely at the top of the tree in governmental circles. So they didn't need to be told what to do because they were anyway of the same mind as the government.

DC. You've touched on a slightly raw nerve there given that I was an under-secretary in the Cabinet and Home Office before I came here. But I resigned when I came here. There's no question of me coming on secondment and going on being a civil servant; my pension was frozen, and I certainly don't regard my background as meaning that I'm somehow acclimatized to what Whitehall wants me to do.

JP. I think that politicians sometimes rather arrogantly think that they'll appoint X or Y because they're going to be malleable, but if appointees are worth their salt they actually identify with the organization to which they've come rather than with the one they've just left. Nonetheless, I maintain that the government would rather you were the director of the BBFC as opposed to me. My point is neither a personal nor a conspiratorial one, it's quite simply that people—all of us who work—know the limits of the possible in our jobs, and that, if we want to keep those jobs, we'd be well advised to stick within those limits whether or not we agree with all of them.

DC. Yes, obviously there are constraints in any job but the way it feels to me is that I couldn't allow 'cunts' in a PG not because I think some minister is going to de-designate Quentin [Sir Quentin Thomas, BBFC President] and me but because that would be a betrayal of what we've agreed with the public with whom we have a contract.

THE BRITISH BOARD OF FILM CLASSIFICATION GUIDELINES

'U' UNIVERSAL—SUITABLE FOR ALL

It is impossible to predict what might upset any particular child. But a 'U' film should be suitable for audiences aged four years and over. 'U' films should be set within a positive moral framework and should offer reassuring counterbalances to any violence, threat or horror.

Videos classified 'Uc' are particularly suitable for pre-school children and normally raise none of the issues set out below.

THEME
Treatment of problematic themes must be sensitive and appropriate for a younger audience.

LANGUAGE

Infrequent use only of very mild bad language.

NUDITY

Occasional natural nudity, with no sexual context.

SEX

Mild sexual behaviour (e.g. kissing) and references only (e.g. to 'making love').

VIOLENCE

Mild violence only. Occasional mild threat or menace only.

IMITABLE TECHNIQUES

No emphasis on realistic or easily accessible weapons. No potentially dangerous behaviour which young children are likely to copy.

HORROR

Horror effects should be mild and brief and should take account of the presence of very young viewers. The outcome should be re-assuring.

DRUGS

No references to illegal drugs or drug misuse

unless there is a clear educational purpose or
clear anti-drug message suitable for the
audience.

'PG' PARENTAL GUIDANCE—GENERAL VIEWING, BUT SOME SCENES MAY BE UNSUITABLE FOR YOUNG CHILDREN

Unaccompanied children of any age may watch.
A 'PG' film should not disturb a child aged
around eight or older. However, parents are advised to consider whether the content may upset
younger or more sensitive children.

THEME
Where more serious issues are featured (e.g. domestic violence, racist abuse), nothing in their
treatment should condone the behaviour.

LANGUAGE
Mild bad language only.

NUDITY
Natural nudity, with no sexual context.

SEX
Sexual activity may be implied, but should be

discreet and infrequent. Mild sex references and innuendo only.

VIOLENCE

Moderate violence, without detail, may be allowed, if justified by its setting (e.g. historic, comedy or fantasy).

IMITABLE TECHNIQUES

No glamorization of realistic or easily accessible weapons. No detail of potentially dangerous behaviour which young children are likely to copy.

HORROR

Frightening sequences should not be prolonged or intense. Fantasy settings may be a mitigating factor.

DRUGS

Any references to illegal drugs or drug misuse must be innocuous or carry a suitable anti-drug message.

12A—SUITABLE FOR 12 YEARS AND OVER

No one younger than 12 may see a '12A' film in a cinema unless accompanied by an adult. No one younger than 12 may rent or buy a '12' rated video or DVD. Responsibility for allowing under-12s to view lies with the accompanying or supervising adult.

THEME

Mature themes are acceptable, but their treatment must be suitable for young teenagers.

LANGUAGE

The use of strong language (e.g. 'fuck') must be infrequent. Racist abuse is also of particular concern.

NUDITY

Nudity is allowed, but in a sexual context must be brief and discreet.

SEX

Sexual activity may be implied. Sex references may reflect what is likely to be familiar to most adolescents but should not go beyond what is suitable for them.

VIOLENCE

Violence must not dwell on detail. There should be no emphasis on injuries or blood. Sexual violence may only be implied or briefly and discreetly indicated.

IMITABLE TECHNIQUES

Dangerous techniques (e.g. combat, hanging, suicide and self-harming) should not dwell on imitable detail or appear pain or harm free. Easily accessible weapons should not be glamorized.

HORROR

Sustained moderate threat and menace are permitted. Occasional gory moments only.

DRUGS

Any misuse of drugs must be infrequent and should not be glamorized or instructional.

'15'—SUITABLE ONLY FOR 15 YEARS AND OVER

No one younger than 15 may see a '15' film in a cinema. No one younger than 15 may rent or buy a '15' rated video or DVD.

THEME

No theme is prohibited, provided the treatment is appropriate to 15 year olds.

LANGUAGE

There may be frequent use of strong language (e.g. 'fuck'). But the strongest terms (e.g. 'cunt') will be acceptable only where justified by the context. Con-

tinued aggressive use of the strongest language is
unlikely to be acceptable.

NUDITY

Nudity may be allowed in a sexual context but
without strong detail. There are no constraints on
nudity in a non-sexual or educational context.

SEX

Sexual activity may be portrayed but without
strong detail. There may be strong verbal references to sexual behaviour.

VIOLENCE

Violence may be strong but may not dwell on the
infliction of pain or injury. Scenes of sexual violence must be discreet and brief.

IMITABLE TECHNIQUES

Dangerous techniques (e.g. combat, hanging, suicide and self-harming) should not dwell on imitable detail. Easily accessible weapons should not
be glamorized.

HORROR

Strong threat and menace are permitted. The
strongest gory images are unlikely to be
acceptable.

DRUGS

Drug-taking may be shown but the film as a whole must not promote or encourage drug misuse.

'18'—SUITABLE ONLY FOR ADULTS

No one younger than 18 may see an '18' film in a cinema. No one younger than 18 may rent or buy an '18' rated video.

In line with the consistent findings of the BBFC's public consultations, at '18' the BBFC's guideline concerns will not normally override the wish that adults should be free to choose their own entertainment, within the law. Exceptions are most likely in the following areas:

—where material or treatment appears to the Board to risk harm to individuals or, through their behaviour, to society—e.g. any detailed portrayal of violent or dangerous acts, or of illegal drug use, which is likely to promote the activity. The Board may also intervene with portrayals of sexual violence which might, for example, eroticize or endorse sexual assault;

—the more explicit images of sexual activity—unless they can be exceptionally justified by context and the work is not a 'sex work' as defined below.

In the case of videos and DVDs, which may be more accessible to younger viewers, intervention may be more frequent. For the same reason, and because of the different ways in which they are experienced, the Board may take a more precautionary approach in the case of those digital games which are covered by the Video Recordings Act.

SEX EDUCATION AT '18'

Where sex material genuinely seeks to inform and educate in matters such as human sexuality, safe sex and health, exceptions to the normal constraints on explicit images may be made in the public interest. Such explicit detail must be kept to the minimum necessary to illustrate the educational or instructional points being made.

SEX WORKS AT '18'

Sex works are works, normally on video or DVD, whose primary purpose is sexual arousal or stimulation. Sex works containing material which may be simulated are generally passed '18', while sex works containing clear images of real sex are confined to the 'R18' category.

'R18'—TO BE SHOWN ONLY IN SPECIALLY LI-CENSED CINEMAS, OR SUPPLIED ONLY IN LI-CENSED SEX SHOPS, AND TO ADULTS OF NOT LESS THAN 18 YEARS.

The 'R18' category is a special and legally restricted classification primarily for explicit works of consenting sex between adults. Films may only be shown to adults in specially licensed cinemas, and videos may be supplied to adults only in licensed sex shops. 'R18' videos may not be supplied by mail order.

The following content is not acceptable:

—any material which is in breach of the criminal law, including material judged to be obscene under the current interpretation of the Obscene Publications Act 1959;

—material (including dialogue) likely to encourage an interest in sexually abusive activity (e.g.

paedophilia, incest, rape) which may include adults role-playing as non-adults;

—the portrayal of any sexual activity which involves lack of consent (whether real or simulated). Any form of physical restraint which prevents participants from indicating a withdrawal of consent;

—the infliction of pain or physical harm, real or (in a sexual context) simulated. Some allowance may be made for mild consensual activity. Penetration by any object likely to cause actual harm or associated with violence;

—any sexual threats, humiliation or abuse which does not form part of a clearly consenting role-playing game. Strong abuse, even if consensual, is unlikely to be acceptable.

These guidelines will be applied to the same standard whether the activity is heterosexual or homosexual.

THE VIDEO RECORDINGS ACT 1984

The Act requires the BBFC to have special regard (among other relevant factors) to the likelihood of works being viewed in the home, and to

—any harm to those likely to view a video;

—any harm to society through the behaviour of those viewers afterwards.

In considering these issues the Board has in mind the possible effect not only on children but also on other vulnerable people.

The Act further requires that special regard is paid to the manner in which the work deals with:

—criminal behaviour

—use of illegal drugs

—violent behaviour or incidents

—horrific behaviour or incidents

—human sexual activity

THE AMERICAN RATINGS SYSTEM, AS EXPLAINED BY THE MOTION PICTURE ASSOCIATION OF AMERICA (MPAA)

The Classification and Ratings Board was created in response to a national cry for some kind of regulation of film content. During the 1960s, the social pressures of an ever-evolving country fostered a sense of concern for the new topics and issues being explored by the creative industries, namely in the movies. The motion picture industry sought to find a balance between preserving creative freedoms and notifying people about films content so that people could make decisions about what movies they wanted to see and what movies were appropriate for their children.

Former president of the MPAA, Jack Valenti worked with the National Association of Theatre

Owners (NATO) to create a new and, at the time, revolutionary approach to fulfilling the movie industry's self-prescribed obligation to the parents of America. On 1 November 1968, NATO, MPAA and IFIDA (International Film Importers and Distributors of America) announced the birth of the new voluntary film-rating system of the motion picture industry. The initial design called for four rating categories:

G for General Audiences, all ages admitted;

M for Mature Audiences, parental guidance suggested but all ages admitted;

R for Restricted, children under 16 not be admitted without an accompanying parent or adult guardian (this was later raised to 17 years of age, and varies in some jurisdictions);

X for no one under 17 admitted.

The rating system trademarked all the category symbols, except the X. Under the plan, anyone who did not submit his or her film for rating could self-apply the X or any other symbol or description, except those trademarked by the rating programme.

The original plan had been to use only three rating categories. Valenti felt that parents ought to be able to accompany their children to any movie the parents choose, without the movie industry, government or self-appointed groups interfering with their rights. But NATO urged the creation of an adult-only category, fearful of possible legal redress under state or local law. Hence, the four-category system, including the X rating, was installed.

Hence, the emergence of the voluntary rating system filled the vacuum provided by the dismantling of the Hays Production Code. The movie industry would no longer disapprove the content of a film, but would now see its primary task as giving advance cautionary warnings to parents so they could make the decision about what movies their children see.

CHANGES IN THE RATING SYSTEM

After the creation of the rating system, the Board found that the M category (mature) was regarded by most parents as a sterner rating than the R (restricted) category. To remedy this misconception, the rating was changed from M to GP (general audiences, parental guidance suggested). A year later, the name was revised to its current label, PG (parental guidance suggested).

In July 1984, the PG category was split into two groups—PG and PG-13. PG-13 meant a higher level of intensity than was to be found in a film rated PG. Over the past years, parents have approved of this amplifying revision in the rating system. In September 1990, two more revisions were announced. First, the Board began giving brief explanations of why a particular film received R ratings. Since, in the opinion of the Ratings Board, R-rated films contain adult material, they believed it would be useful for parents to know a little more about that film's content before they allowed their children to accompany them. Sometime later, the Board began applying the same explanations in the PG, PG-13 and NC-17 categories as well. These explanations are available to parents at the theatre (by telephone or at the box office), in certain media reviews and listings, and are made available at www.mpaa.org and filmratings.com.

The second change was in the X category, which then became NC-17 (no one 17 and under admitted). The X rating over the years appeared to have taken on a surly meaning in the minds of many people, something that was never intended when the system was created. Therefore, the board chose to reaffirm the original intent of the design that was installed on 1 November 1968, in which the adults-only category explicitly describes a movie that most parents would want to have barred to viewing by their children. These ratings were all trademarked and can only be used for film ratings.

A **G-rated** motion picture contains nothing in theme, language, nudity, sex, violence or other matters that, in the view of the Ratings Board, would offend parents whose younger children view the motion picture. The G rating is not a 'certificate of approval', nor does it signify a 'children's' motion picture. Some snippets of language may go beyond polite conversation but they are common everyday expressions. No stronger words are present in G-rated motion pictures. Depictions of violence are minimal. No nudity, sex scenes or drug use is present in the motion picture.

A **PG-rated** motion picture should be investigated by parents before they let their younger children attend. The PG rating indicates, in the view of the Ratings Board, that parents may consider some material unsuitable for their children, and parents should make that decision.

The more mature themes in some PG-rated motion pictures may call for parental guidance. There may be some profanity and some depictions of violence or brief nudity. But these elements are not deemed so intense as to require that parents be strongly cautioned beyond the suggestion of parental guidance. There is no drug use content in a PG-rated motion picture.

A **PG-13** rating is a sterner warning by the Ratings Board to parents to determine whether their children under age 13 should view the motion picture, as some material might not be suited for them. A PG-13 motion picture may go beyond the PG rating in theme, violence, nudity, sensuality, language, adult activities or other elements, but does not reach the restricted R category. The theme of the motion picture by itself will not result in a rating greater than PG-13, although depictions of activities related to a mature theme may result in a restricted rating for the motion picture. Any drug use will initially require at least a PG-13 rating. More than brief

censoring the moving image

nudity will require at least a PG-13 rating, but such nudity in a PG-13-rated motion picture generally will not be sexually oriented. There may be depictions of violence in a PG-13 movie, but generally not both realistic and extreme or persistent violence. A motion picture's single use of one of the harsher sexually derived words, though only as an expletive, initially requires at least a PG-13 rating. More than one such expletive requires an R rating, as must even one of those words used in a sexual context. The Ratings Board nevertheless may rate such a motion picture PG-13 if, based on a special vote by a two-thirds majority, the Raters feel that most American parents would believe that a PG-13 rating is appropriate because of the context or manner in which the words are used or because the use of those words in the motion picture is inconspicuous.

An **R-rated** motion picture, in the view of the Ratings Board, contains some adult material. An R-rated motion picture may include adult themes, adult activity, hard language, intense or persistent violence, sexually oriented nudity, drug abuse or other elements, so that parents are counselled to take this rating very seriously. Children under 17 are not allowed to attend R-rated motion pictures unaccompanied by a parent or adult guardian. Parents are strongly urged to find out more about R-rated motion pictures in determining their suitability for their children. Generally, it is not appropriate for parents to bring their young children with them to R-rated motion pictures.

An **NC-17**-rated motion picture is one that, in the view of the Ratings Board, most parents would consider patently too adult for their children 17 and under. No children will be admitted. NC-17 does not mean 'obscene' or 'pornographic' in the common or legal meaning of those words, and should not be construed as a negative judgement in any sense. The rating simply signals that the content is appropriate only for an adult audience. An NC-17 rating can be based on violence, sex, aberrational behaviour, drug abuse or any other element that most parents would consider too strong and therefore off-limits for viewing by their children.

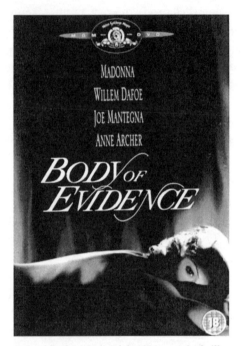

Body of Evidence (Uli Edel, 1992): erotic thriller starring Madonna, a victim of the NC-17 rating system.

BIBLIOGRAPHY

Barker, Martin. 1984. *The Video Nasties*: *Freedom and Censorship in the Media*. London: Pluto Press.

Barker, Martin and Julian Petley. 2001. *Ill Effects*: *the Media Violence Debate*. London: Routledge (second edition).

Barker, Martin, Jane Arthurs and Ramaswami Harindranath. 2001. *The Crash Controversy*: *Censorship Campaigns and Film Reception*. London: Wallflower Press.

Black, Gregory D. 1996. *Hollywood Censored*: *Morality Codes, Catholics and the Movies*. Cambridge: Cambridge University Press.

——. 1998. *The Catholic Crusade Against the Movies, 1940–1975*. Cambridge: Cambridge University Press.

Home Office. 1979. *Report of the Committee on Obscenity and Film Censorship*. London: Her Majesty's Stationery Office.

Kerekes, David and David Slater. 2000. *See No Evil*: *Banned Films and Video Controversy*. Manchester: Critical Vision/Headpress.

LEFF, Leonard J. and Gerald L Simmons. 2001. *The Dame in the Kimono*: *Hollywood, Censorship and the Production Code*. Kentucky: University Press of Kentucky.

LEWIS, Jon. 2000. *Hollywood v Hard Core*: *How the Struggle Over Pornography Created the Modern Film Industry*. New York: New York University Press.

LYONS, Charles. 1997. *The New Censors*: *Movies and the Culture Wars*. Philadelphia: Temple University Press.

MARTIN, John. 1997. *Seduction of the Gullible*: *the Truth Behind the Video Nasty Scandal*. Milwaukee: Procrustes Press (second edition).

MATHEWS, Tom Dewe. 1994. *Censored*: *What They Didn't Allow You to See and Why: the Story of Film Censorship in Britain*, London: Chatto and Windus.

MILLER, Frank. 1995. *Censored Hollywood*: *Sex, Sin and Violence on Screen*. Maine: Turner Publishing.

PETLEY, Julian and Mark Kermode. 1997. 'Road Rage'. *Sight and Sound* (June issue), London: British Film Institute.

PHELPS, Guy. 1975. *Film Censorship*. London: Victor Gollancz.

ROBERTSON, James C. 1993. *The Hidden Cinema*: *British Film Censorship in Action 1913–72*. London: Routledge.

TREVELYAN, John. 1973. *What the Censor Saw*. London: Michael Joseph.